Great Minds of Science

William Harvey

Discoverer of How Blood Circulates

Revised Edition

Lisa Yount

Enslow Publishers, Inc.
40 Industrial Road
Box 398
Berkeley Heights, NJ 07922
USA

http://www.enslow.com

To Harry,
with all my heart

Library of Congress Cataloging-in-Publication Data

Yount, Lisa.
  William Harvey : discoverer of how blood circulates / Lisa Yount.—Rev. ed.
     p. cm.—(Great minds of science)
  Summary: "A biography of seventeenth-century English physician William
Harvey and includes related activities for readers"—Provided by publisher.
  Includes bibliographical references and index.
  ISBN-13: 978-0-7660-3010-7
  ISBN-10: 0-7660-3010-5
  1. Harvey, William, 1578-1657—Juvenile literature. 2. Physiologists—
England—Biography—Juvenile literature. 3. Physicians—England—
Biography—Juvenile literature. 4. Blood—Circulation—History—Juvenile
literature. I. Title.
  QP26.H3Y68 2008
  610.92—dc22
  [B]
                                    2007020301

Printed in the United States of America

10 9 8 7 6 5 4 3 2 1

✿ Enslow Publishers, Inc., is committed to printing our books on recycled
paper. The paper in every book contains 10% to 30% post-consumer waste
(PCW). The cover board on the outside of each book contains 100% PCW. Our
goal is to do our part to help young people and the environment too!

Illustration Credits: Kim Austin/Enslow Publishers, Inc., pp. 38, 41, 46, 68, 76,
106; The Granger Collection, New York, pp. 53, 60, 64; History of Medicine
Division, National Library of Medicine, pp. 29, 31, 88, 91, 104;
iStockphoto.com/Guy Erwood, p. 81; Johns Hopkins Institute of the History of
Medicine, pp. 9, 84
Jupiterimages Corporation/Photos.com, pp. 58, 78; Life Art Image copyright
1998 Lippincott Williams & Wilkins. All rights reserved., pp. 44, 115; Mayo
Clinic, p. 6; Philadelphia Museum of Art: SmithKline Beckman Corporation
Fund, p. 26; Royal College of Physicians of London, p. 21; SSPL/The Image
Works, pp. 11, 19; Visual Arts Library (London)/Alamy, p. 97.

Cover Illustration: iStockphoto.com/Jasminam (background); Visual Arts
Library (London)/Alamy (inset).

Contents

Introduction: Mending the Heart

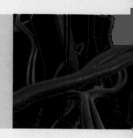

SURGEONS GATHER AROUND THE MAN on the operating table. They are ready to start the operation.

The chief surgeon cuts open the man's chest. She sees his heart jump and quiver like a frightened bird. Faster than once a second it squeezes together, then relaxes. Each time it squeezes, it forces blood through the man's body.

Several large blood vessels connect to the heart. The surgeon ties strings called sutures around two of them. This stops the blood flow. Then she cuts the vessels below the tied part. She joins the cut ends to a machine and takes the strings off. Now the man's blood flows through the machine. It is called a heart-lung machine because it does the work of the man's heart and

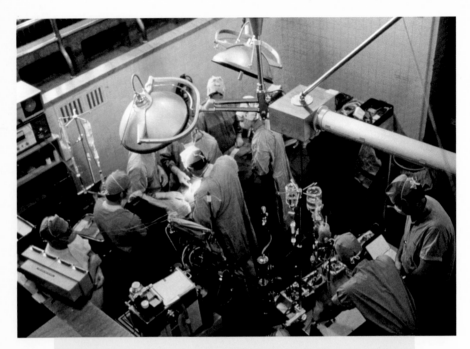

Surgeons can save lives today because of what William Harvey learned about the heart.

lungs during the operation. It will put oxygen into his blood, as the lungs do. Then it will pump the blood back into his body. The heart, too, is a pump, moving blood around the body.

The surgeon uses a drug to stop the man's heart. Slowly the jumping and quivering cease. Now she and her assistants repair the heart. They may replace vessels near the heart that have been blocked by disease. They may repair or replace valves in the heart. When healthy, these valves control the way the blood flows through the heart. Diseased valves may partly block blood flow or allow the blood to travel in the wrong direction.

When the surgeon is finished, she rejoins the cut blood vessels to the heart. Then she lets blood flow through the man's heart again. The blood washes out the drug, and the heart starts to beat once more.

Four hundred years ago, such an operation would have been impossible. Doctors then knew little about the heart and blood. In 1628, a man named William Harvey changed everything. Harvey's discoveries form the base of what we now know about the heart and blood vessels. For this reason, the man on the operating table owes his life to more than his surgeon. He also owes it to William Harvey.

Learning to Be a Doctor

WILLIAM HARVEY WAS BORN ON APRIL 1, 1578, in a stone house in Folkestone, England. His parents were Thomas Harvey and Harvey's second wife, Joan. William was the first of what one writer called "a week of sons" (that is, seven of them) born to the Harveys.[1] The couple also had two daughters.

Childhood in the Country

Folkestone is in the part of southern England called Kent. Kent is a land of woods, grass-covered hills, and deep, narrow valleys. Only the sheep that graze there seem fitted to walk on its narrow tracks. Harvey's father owned a farm called West Dane, so young William no doubt saw the countryside often. He must have liked

William Harvey was one of Thomas Harvey's seven sons. William is in the upper right of this group of family portraits. The large portrait in the center shows Thomas Harvey.

studying the many plants and animals that lived there. All his life he wanted to learn about living things.

Folkestone itself made people think of ships instead of sheep. It was a small coastal town. Most people there fished for a living. Large ships had once visited Folkestone, but by William

Harvey's time, sand had made the harbor too shallow for them. A ruined castle on a hill reminded people of the town's lost glory.

William's childhood was comfortable. His father, Thomas, was a well-to-do merchant and sheep farmer who also ran the town post office. The people of Folkestone admired Thomas Harvey enough to elect him mayor in 1586.

William entered King's School in Canterbury when he was ten. This school claimed to be one of the two oldest in England. William stayed there for four years. Among other things, he learned Latin and Greek. All educated people were supposed to know these ancient languages. William and the other boys had to speak them even when they were playing.

William had relatives in Canterbury. He probably lived with them when he went to King's School. One is thought to have been an apothecary. (An apothecary was a tradesman who made medicines for doctors.) If William stayed with him, the boy's love of medicine may have begun at that time.

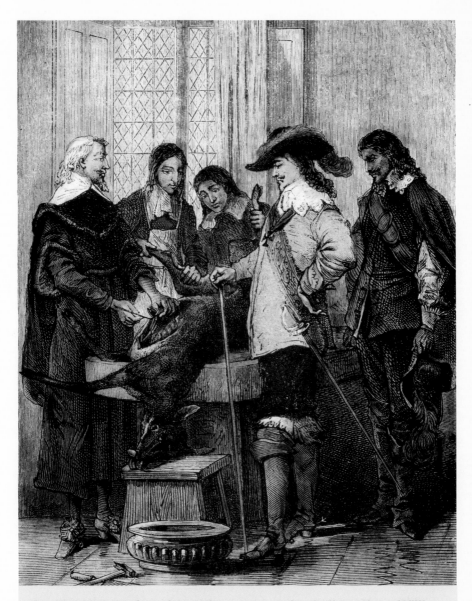

An illustration of a sixteenth-century animal dissection. William Harvey's own study of dissected bodies would later lead to amazing new discoveries about the body and circulation.

College Days

In 1593, at sixteen years old, William Harvey moved on to Gonville and Caius College. This college was part of Cambridge University. It had once been called Gonville Hall. "Caius" was added when John Caius, a rich physician, gave money to make it larger.

Harvey never wrote about his life in Cambridge. The writing of others, though, suggests what it must have been like. Students had to go to church at five o'clock in the morning. Classes started at ten minutes past six. After four hours, at about ten, the students had a dinner (midday meal) of meat, soup, and oatmeal. Then they went on "teaching or learning" until five o'clock. They had a supper "not much better than their dinner."[2] They did homework until nine or ten.

Students lived at the school. Three or four shared each room. The rooms had no heat. Many students walked or ran for half an hour before bedtime to warm up a little before they went to sleep.

College life was not all work. Cambridge students loved to play football. (The British version of football is similar to American soccer.) William Harvey surely would have learned this game at King's School. He also may have joined other students in watching the plays that strolling actors performed in the streets of the town.

Most of Harvey's studies during his first few years at Cambridge were not directly related to medicine. Most likely he took classes in rhetoric (writing and public speaking). He would have studied ethics, logic (reasoning), and philosophy (the rules of nature and human actions). He would have had classes in religion as well. (Harvey, like most English people of his time, belonged to the Anglican Church, or Church of England.) Mathematics and music probably were part of his studies, too. He may have taken a course in the physical sciences. All these subjects were taught to most college students in Harvey's day. Some of them later helped Harvey write convincing explanations of his discoveries.

Harvey received his bachelor of arts degree from Cambridge in 1597. He then began his medical studies. His classes would have seemed very strange to a student of today because most of the information in them came from thinkers of ancient Greece and Rome. The most important medical writer was Galen, who had lived in the Roman Empire in the second century A.D. This meant that Harvey's main textbook was more than fourteen hundred years old!

Few people had dared to question anything Galen wrote. Sometimes a dissection showed something different from what Galen had described. When that happened, Harvey's teachers just said that human bodies must have changed since Galen's time.

Galen himself probably would have been angry to hear such statements. He had written, "The surest judge of all will be experience alone."[3] Harvey came to agree with Galen that scientists should learn about the world by using their own senses, not by depending on what others said. Scientists today work this way. In Harvey's day, however, this important part of Galen's wisdom had been mostly forgotten.

Harvey most likely did receive one piece of practical training at Cambridge. Dr. Caius had arranged for the college to receive the bodies of two executed criminals each year. Teachers dissected, or cut up, the bodies while Harvey and the other students watched. In this way, the students learned about the body's structure. The study of the body's structure is called anatomy.

Eye-Opening Teachers

William Harvey went to the University of Padua for advanced medical training in 1600. At the time, Padua belonged to Venice. Venice, in turn, was one of many separate city-states that made up what is now Italy.

Padua's university was one of the best in Europe for a doctor-to-be. Unlike most other universities in Europe, the one at Padua was not run by a church. Students of all religious backgrounds went there, and they even helped choose their teachers and run the university. They were divided into twenty-two "nations," according to the countries they came from. Each nation chose one or two students to join the governing body. The English nation chose William Harvey three years in a row.

The teacher who meant the most to Harvey was his anatomy teacher, Fabricius. Fabricius, an Italian, was famous. He was nearly seventy years old when Harvey came to Padua. Harvey may have chosen Padua because he knew that expert anatomy professors like Fabricius taught there.

Like Galen before and Harvey after him, Fabricius believed that students should learn by seeing for themselves. He almost surely told his classes about an earlier Padua professor, Andreas Vesalius, who had thought the same thing. Vesalius, born in what is now Belgium but was then part of Holland, had begun teaching at Padua in 1537.

Vesalius performed his own dissections and found many mistakes in anatomy that Galen had made. He began to suspect that Galen had never dissected human beings at all. Instead, the Roman had made guesses about human anatomy based on dissections of apes.

With the help of an artist, Vesalius prepared an illustrated book of human anatomy. Published in 1543, the book became famous at once. It shocked many professors, though, because it dared to question Galen. Vesalius left Padua abruptly the year after his book appeared.

By Harvey's time, Vesalius's ideas were more accepted—at least in Padua. Learning about Vesalius showed Harvey, perhaps for the first time, that Galen could be wrong. If Galen had made mistakes in anatomy, Harvey began to think, the Roman expert might also have misunderstood the way the body works.

Learning About the Body

Fabricius did more dissections than the teachers at Cambridge. In 1594 he had built a special anatomy classroom to let students see the dissections more clearly. It had five circles, or galleries, one above the other. Three hundred students could stand in the galleries. The students in each gallery could see easily over the heads of those below. Fabricius's classroom still exists, and visitors can tour it.

Fabricius dissected animals as well as human bodies. He believed that students should compare the anatomies of different living things. William Harvey came to share this belief. Fabricius also worked with fetuses, or unborn living things. He used them to show how animals developed before birth. This subject, which Fabricius was one of the first people to study, also fascinated Harvey.

Harvey remembered one of Fabricius's lessons all his life. It was about the valves in a body's veins. The veins are one of two kinds of tubes, or vessels, that carry blood. (Arteries are the other kind.) Fabricius claimed he was the first to notice tiny flaps that stick out from the walls of these blood vessels. He called the flaps "little doors." He saw that they could block or at least slow the flow of blood through the veins.

These "little doors" later helped Harvey

Fabricius designed his own anatomy classroom at the University of Padua. He arranged it so all his students could see his dissections clearly. The students stood in five circular galleries, one above the other.

understand how blood moves through the body. Fabricius, however, did not guess the meaning of his own discovery. He described the movement of the blood by repeating what Galen had written about it.

Fabricius's classes were not Harvey's only medical training. Medical students also went to hospitals near the school and studied sick people. Harvey later wrote about cancers and other diseases he had seen in Padua's hospitals. Fabricius sometimes cut open the bodies of people who had died in the hospitals to show students the effects of different diseases.

William Harvey graduated from the University of Padua on April 25, 1602. The graduation ceremony was described in his diploma. The professor of medicine gave Harvey "certain books of philosophy and of medicine, first closed and then . . . open." He then put a gold ring on Harvey's finger and placed a doctor's cap on Harvey's head. Finally, he blessed Harvey and gave him "the kiss of peace."[4]

The first page of Harvey's diploma from the University of Padua shows his personal emblem at the top. The candle reminds us of the new light he brought to medical science.

Harvey's diploma can still be seen at the headquarters of the Royal College of Physicians in London. The diploma has hand-painted lettering and colored decorations. At the top of the first page is the emblem, or coat of arms, that Harvey chose for himself. The emblem shows a white-sleeved arm holding a lighted candle against a red backgound. Two green snakes twine around the candle. Snakes were the symbol of Aesculapius, the Roman god of medicine. Harvey's emblem was a fitting one. In years to come, he would bring new light to medical science.

Harvey the Physician

AFTER WILLIAM HARVEY FINISHED HIS studies in Padua, he went back to England. There he received an M.D. (doctor of medicine) degree from Cambridge in 1602. Cambridge required study at places like Padua before granting its own degree.

Harvey wanted to work as a medical doctor in London. That meant he needed a license from the city's Royal College of Physicians. The Royal College was not a school but a group of powerful doctors, set up in 1518. Part of its job was to "counsel [advise] and govern those who practiced medicine in London."[1] It was supposed to make sure that only doctors with good medical training treated sick people.

Before giving Harvey a license, doctors from

the Royal College asked him questions. He had to say how he would identify and treat different diseases. (Doctors today still must take licensing tests before beginning to practice medicine.) The doctors liked Harvey's answers and granted his license in October 1604. Three years later he became a member of the Royal College.

By this time, Harvey was a mature young man. His appearance most likely was not too different from what descriptions and pictures show for him when he was older. John Aubrey, a friend who knew Harvey late in life, wrote that Harvey was "of the lowest stature [height], round faced, olivaster [olive-skinned] . . . in complexion, [had a] little eye, round, very black, full of spirit; his hair was black as a raven."[2]

Starting a Career

Soon after gaining his license, twenty-six-year-old Dr. Harvey married a woman named Elizabeth Browne. The two took out a marriage license on November 24, 1604, and were wed soon after. Nothing is known about Harvey's home life, but he may have had a happy marriage because he is thought to have said, "A blessing goes with a marriage for love."[3] Harvey and his wife had no children.

Elizabeth Harvey's father was named Lancelot Browne. Like Harvey, Browne was a physician. Browne worked at the court of Queen Elizabeth I. After the queen's death in 1603, he stayed at court and became one of the doctors for the new king, James I.

Browne must have liked his new son-in-law. In 1605 he tried to get Harvey a job as a physician in the Tower of London. "I did never in my life know any man anything near his years that was . . . [a] match with him in . . . learning," Browne wrote of Harvey.[4] Even so, an older doctor won the job. In that year, too, both Harvey's mother and his helpful father-in-law died.

Harvey's brother John was also serving in King James's court. Like Lancelot Browne, John no doubt introduced William Harvey to people at court. Harvey soon began to collect patients

L'INFIRMERIE DE L'HOSPITAL DE LA CHARITE DE PARIS.

Vous aurez beaucoup merité,   Vous voyez combien ardammant   Ils font toute forte defforts,   Jmitant leurs foings genereux,
Pour jouyr des chofes profperes;   Leur propre Vertu les oblige   Dont vn zele faint les enflamme;   Vous deux employer vos peines
Si vous fuivez la CHARITE,   A Secourir a tout moment   Et pour la guerifon du Corps,   A feruir les Pauures comme eux
Qu'exercent icy ces bons Peres.   Ceux que la Maladie affige   Ils penfent au falut de l'Ame   Dans les infirmitez humaines

Harvey became the physician of St. Batholomew's Hospital in London. The hospital's main hall probably looked much like the one in this Paris hospital.

who belonged to the nobility. His quick mind and lively manner must have impressed them. In October 1609, Harvey became the physician of St. Bartholomew's Hospital, a large hospital near his home. It was one of the two hospitals in London that cared for poor people.

St. Bartholomew's could hold over two hundred patients. They stayed in twelve large rooms, or wards. Thirteen nurses took care of them. Three surgeons also worked for the hospital, and a hospital apothecary made medicines. Harvey, as physician, was in charge of all these other workers.

Harvey went to St. Bartholomew's at least one day a week. The patients who needed a doctor's help were brought to him in the hospital's Great Hall. He examined each one, then wrote orders for the person's treatment. He might tell a surgeon to operate. He might order certain drugs from the apothecary. Harvey also looked at new patients and those ready to go home.

Work for the Royal College

Harvey also spent a lot of time with the Royal College of Physicians. In years to come, he would hold all the high offices in this group except president.

Every other year, starting in 1616, Harvey gave talks or lectures to the Royal College. The lectures, held each Wednesday and Friday, described anatomy and surgery. A man named John Lumley had given money to start the lectures in 1582, so they were called the Lumleian Lectures. Harvey gave these talks until 1643.

Each winter Harvey dissected a body as part of his lectures. He talked about it for an hour a day for three to five days. He spent the first day on the abdomen or "lower belly." He said it was "nasty yet recompensed [made up for] by admirable variety." On the second day, he cut open the chest to show the heart, lungs, and large blood vessels. The third day was devoted to "the divine banquet [feast] of the brain."[5]

We know something about what Harvey said in his talks because his lecture notes were found in 1876. The notes mention things he saw during dissections and while treating patients. They describe the structure and actions of body parts. They compare healthy parts with those changed by disease. They also compare human

Harvey dissected a body for the Royal College of Physicians each winter. This picture shows a similar dissection at a medical school.

bodies with those of animals, mentioning more than one hundred kinds of animals.

Most important, Harvey's notes show him following in the footsteps of Vesalius and Fabricius. They describe his progress in developing the ideas that would make him famous. In the introduction to his book on the heart, Harvey said he had shown his discoveries to the Royal College in his lectures for more than nine years.

Besides giving lectures, Harvey helped interview people accused of practicing medicine without the Royal College's permission. The Royal College tried hard to prevent such a practice. This was partly because it wanted to protect sick people from untrained "doctors," who could do a lot of harm. The college also wanted to protect its own power. It was the only group in London that could give out medical licenses. As long as all London doctors had to have such licenses, the Royal College could control medicine in the city.

Many people accused of practicing medicine

without a license were barber-surgeons or apothecaries. (The short red-and-white striped pole that used to be placed outside barber shops was a reminder of the long-ago days when barbers also performed bloody operations.) The Royal College claimed that these groups had less

medical training than physicians. Most did not know Latin as physicians did, for example. For this reason, the Royal College said, such people should not do a physician's work. For instance, they should not prescribe medicines. (Physicians could both perform surgery and make drugs, however.)

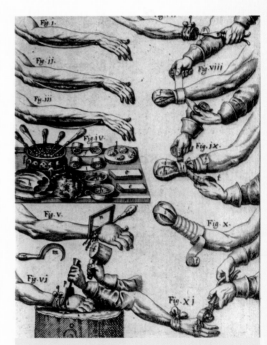

These pictures show how barber-surgeons of Harvey's time might cut off a diseased hand. Some barber-surgeons were very skilled, but they were supposed to take their orders from physicians.

In fact, the best surgeons and apothecaries probably were as good as the physicians at treating sick people. They formed their own professional groups, which were as powerful as the Royal College, and they fought against the physicians' control. The battle between the physicians and these other groups continued long after Harvey's death.

Some people practiced medicine without any training at all. They were often called "quacks," a term of disrespect in Harvey's time as well as our own. Most of their treatments were useless, and some were dangerous. Still, these fake doctors were not all bad. They brought some kind of medical care to the many people who could not afford physicians. Some stayed to do business during disease epidemics, when most doctors left town.

Harvey as a Doctor

To a modern eye, many of the physicians' treatments would seem just as senseless or dangerous as those of the quacks. Most doctors of Harvey's time thought people grew sick because they had the wrong amounts of body fluids called humors. This idea came from ancient Greece. In the body of a healthy person, the Greeks believed, the four humors existed in equal amounts. If someone had too much of one of the humors, he or she would become ill.

Doctors tried to restore a healthy balance among the humors by changing the amounts of the fluids. One common treatment was taking blood from the sick person. (Blood was one of the four humors. The others were mucus or phlegm, yellow bile, and black bile.) One doctor said that bleeding should go on "until the patient faints."[6] Such treatments weakened patients and may even have killed a few before disease did.

For his time, William Harvey was a rather old-fashioned doctor. He did not trust new drugs. He used the same treatments other doctors did. His discoveries did not make him change them. For example, his finding that blood was used over and over did not make him stop bleeding people. He did give his patients good advice, however. He told one sick man to "renew his cheerful conversation and take moderate walks for exercise."[7] He told another to eat small meals and avoid alcohol. Doctors still recommend these things. Harvey's avoidance of strong medicines also was often wise.

John Aubrey wrote that people admired Harvey as a scientist but not as a doctor. The fact that Harvey had so many wealthy patients suggested that Aubrey may have been wrong. Harvey's patients even included two kings.

By 1618, King James I was one of Harvey's patients. Harvey was not the king's regular doctor. He was called in only when the king wanted to see him, and he may not have seen the king often. James did not think much of doctors. James's chief doctor wrote, "The King laughs at medicine. . . . He declares physicians to be of very little use."[8] Harvey, in turn, may not have liked King James's court. The king and his friends liked to sing loud songs and play jokes on each other. Harvey was too dignified for that.

Harvey did help take care of King James when the king became ill in 1625. James died on

March 27, probably because his kidneys failed. Some people said, however, that the king had been poisoned. They blamed the Duke of Buckingham, James's close friend.

Parliament looked into King James's death. (Parliament is Britain's lawmaking body. It is like the U.S. Congress.) In April 1626, Parliament investigators asked Harvey and the king's other doctors for a report. Harvey said that Buckingham had given King James a drink. No one was sure what was in it. The king was already very ill by then, though, and no one could prove that the drink had done him any harm. Harvey's report helped clear Buckingham's name.

King James's son, Charles, became Charles I. He kept Harvey as a court physician. Later Harvey would become King Charles's chief doctor and good friend.

Movement of the Heart and Blood

A SMALL BOOK WAS PUBLISHED IN Frankfurt, Germany, in 1628. It was just sixty-eight pages long. The book was written in Latin. (It is often known by the first three words of its Latin title, *De Motu Cordis*—"on the movement of the heart.") In English, its title was *An Anatomical Essay on the Movement of the Heart and Blood in Animals*. Its author was "William Harvey, Englishman."

This little book was printed on cheap paper and was full of misprints. It did not look like something that would change medical science—but that was what it was.

Harvey was fifty years old when his book was printed. He had been thinking about the ideas in it for years. He had mentioned some of them in his lectures. He had talked them over with other doctors at the Royal College.

Some of the doctors had scolded Harvey because his ideas disagreed with those of ancient scientists such as Galen. Surely, the doctors said, he must be wrong. Other doctors, however, liked what he had to say. They wanted to know more. Harvey wrote his book to explain his beliefs clearly to both groups.

Most science books of Harvey's time "proved" their ideas by quoting ancient thinkers. Harvey's book quoted these thinkers, too, but he proved his ideas by telling what he himself had seen. Some of his evidence came from dissections of human bodies. Other evidence came from dissections of dead and living animals. Harvey mentioned over eighty kinds of animals in his book. Few scientists before him had used animals to learn about the human body.

The Heart

The first part of Harvey's book explained how the heart moved. Understanding that

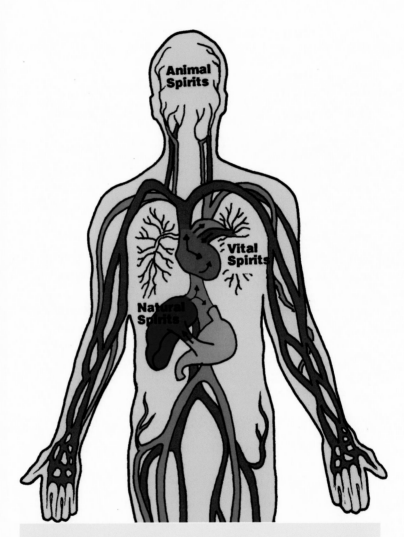

Galen thought there were two kinds of blood. Both flowed into the body and were used up. He also thought the liver, heart, and brain added different kinds of life-giving substances, or spirits, to the blood.

movement had been hard, Harvey wrote. At first he was "tempted to think . . . that the motion of the heart was only to be comprehended by God."[1] The hearts of dogs and deer beat very fast. Harvey said each beat was "like a flash of lightning."[2] He could not see what happened during the beats, so he looked at the hearts of snakes instead. Those hearts beat more slowly. He studied the hearts of dying animals because their hearts beat slowly, too.

Earlier writers had described the parts of the heart. In mammals, the heart has four hollow chambers, or rooms. A solid wall divides the left chambers from the right ones. The upper two chambers are called atria. (*Atria* is a plural word. The singular is *atrium*.) The lower two are ventricles. The ventricles are larger than the atria and have thicker walls.

A small opening connects each atrium with the ventricle below. In each opening is a valve, like a door that opens only one way. The valve makes sure that the blood flows in just one direction. Blood always moves from the atria to the ventricles.

Large blood vessels connect to the heart's chambers. Veins come into the atria. Arteries lead away from the ventricles.

The upper and lower venae cavae, the two biggest veins in the body, come into the right atrium. Four pulmonary (lung) veins come into the left atrium. The pulmonary artery leaves the right ventricle. The aorta leaves the left ventricle. The aorta is the body's largest artery.

All these blood vessels also have valves where they join the heart. The valves in the veins let blood flow only into the heart. Those in the arteries let blood flow only out of the heart. (All the veins in the body have valves, but the only arteries with valves are the arteries attached to the heart.)

How the Heart Works

Earlier scientists thought the heart pulled blood into itself by swelling, or dilating. In this view, the heart would be like an eyedropper. When you squeeze the dropper's bulb and then let go,

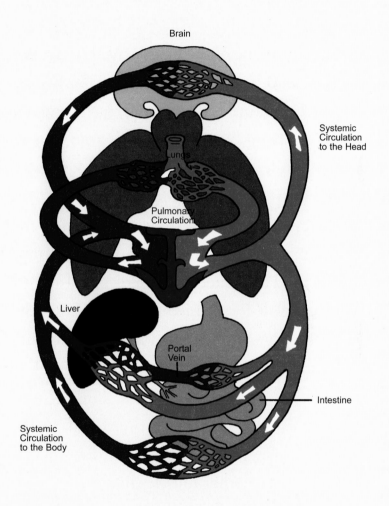

Brain

Systemic
Circulation
to the Head

Lungs

Pulmonary
Circulation

Liver

Portal
Vein

Intestine

Systemic
Circulation
to the Body

Harvey showed that blood moves in circles through the body. One circle goes through the lungs. Red blood vessels carry blood that contains oxygen. Oxygen has been removed from the blood in the blue vessels.

the bulb expands. Liquid is pulled into the tube attached to the bulb.

Harvey was one of the first scientists to realize that the heart is a muscle. Muscles move your body by squeezing and relaxing. For example, when you bend your arm, one arm muscle squeezes while another relaxes. Harvey showed that the heart works the same way.

Harvey discovered that squeezing, or contracting, is the heart's most important movement. This squeezing forces blood out of the heart. You force juice from an orange by squeezing in much the same way. The squeezing also causes the heartbeat. As the heart muscle squeezes, the heart becomes longer and narrower. Part of it moves forward and strikes the chest wall. The heart feels harder when it contracts, just as other muscles do.

The whole heart appears to contract at once. Harvey showed, though, that the atria contract just before the ventricles. (The right and left atria contract together. So do the right and left ventricles.) Harvey said that this quick set of actions is like swallowing. Several muscles are involved in swallowing, and they do different things. Still, swallowing looks like a single action. Harvey also compared the beating heart to a machine with many parts that work together.

Harvey worked out the whole pattern of the heartbeat. The beat starts in the right atrium. (Today we know that a bundle of nerves in this spot controls the heartbeat. This bundle is called the pacemaker.) When the atria contract, they force blood into the ventricles. Then the ventricles contract and push blood into the arteries. Next, the heart muscle relaxes and dilates. Blood pours into the atria from the veins. Then, a second later, the cycle starts again. Harvey said the heart works like a water pump. Such pumps were new in his time. Knowing how these machines work appears to have helped him understand the heart.

You can feel a pulse, or beat, in the arteries of your wrist. Galen thought the arteries pulsed by themselves. He also thought that the arteries pulled blood into themselves by dilating. Harvey

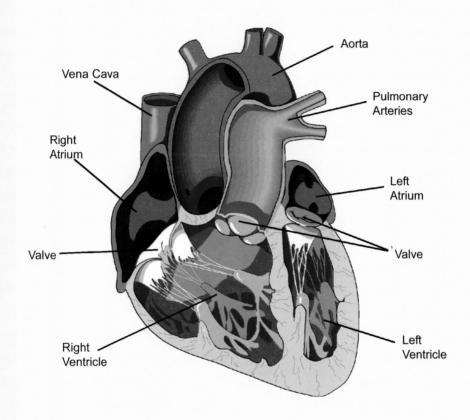

Galen believed there were pores in the heart that allowed blood to move from the right side to the left side. Harvey showed that no such pores exist. The illustration above is a modern view of the heart.

showed that both ideas were wrong. The pulse comes from the heart. The "beat" happens when the heart contracts. The arteries swell because the heart pushes blood into them. In the same way, Harvey said, blowing air into a glove makes the glove's fingers swell.

Galen thought the heart's center wall had tiny holes, or pores, in it. He wrote that blood leaked from the heart's right side to the left side through these pores. Harvey said this was nonsense. "By Hercules! No such pores . . . exist," he announced quite firmly.[3] He agreed, though, that blood must get from the right to the left side of the heart somehow.

The lungs are the answer to this puzzle, Harvey said. Galen and others had seen that blood from the right ventricle goes to the lungs. The pulmonary artery carries it. Most thought, however, that this blood did not return. Its only job was to nourish the lungs. Harvey pointed out that the right ventricle and its blood vessels are just as big as those on the left. Why should the lungs need as much blood as all the rest of

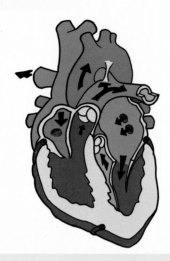

Blood in the heart always flows from the atria to the ventricles. Valves make sure the blood flows in only one direction.

the body, he asked. Why should they need a separate chamber of the heart to pump it?

Harvey said that the blood makes a circle through the lungs. It returns to the left atrium through the pulmonary veins. Other writers had guessed that the blood might do this, but they had not made such a clear statement about it. They also had not offered proof.

One indirect proof of his idea, Harvey said, could be found in unborn babies. Before birth, a human baby does not use its lungs. Its pulmonary artery is joined to its aorta by a short tube. This tube normally closes when the baby is born. Then the blood is forced into the lungs instead of into the aorta.

Harvey was not sure how blood got from

arteries to veins inside the lungs. He guessed that it moved through tiny holes in the lungs or through blood vessels. In fact, very small vessels connect the arteries and the veins. They are called capillaries. Harvey would have needed a microscope to see them. Microscopes were new in Harvey's time, and he did not use one.

Harvey made a mistake in guessing why the blood had to go through the lungs. He thought the lungs cooled the blood. Scientists before him had thought this, too. In fact, the blood goes to the lungs to pick up oxygen from the air. The body's cells need oxygen to live. This element was not discovered until over one hundred years after Harvey's death.

The first half of Harvey's book described his ideas about the heart and arteries. He also told about blood circulation through the lungs. Some historians think Harvey wrote this part of the book years before he wrote the second half. Most of the ideas in the first half of the book are in his lecture notes. Although other scientists also had some of these ideas, no one had put them all together as clearly as Harvey did.

Blood Moves in a Circle

The idea that Harvey presented in the second half of his book was all new. Indeed, he said, it was "so . . . unheard-of that I not only fear injury to myself from the envy of a few, but I tremble lest I have mankind at large for my enemies" because of it. Yet he published it because of his "love of truth."[4]

Harvey tried to find out what happened to blood once it left the heart. Galen and other early scientists believed that blood flowed into the body and was quickly used up. Harvey suspected that they were wrong. Galen had written that the liver made blood from food. Veins carried this dark, nourishing blood through the body, he said. Some of the blood went to the heart and lungs. The heart warmed the blood it received. It also added "vital spirit" to the blood. Vital spirit was made from air breathed in by the lungs. The warmth and vital spirit made the blood turn bright red. This red blood flowed into the arteries from the left ventricle. The arteries carried the red blood into the body. Galen thought that, once in the body, both red and dark blood were quickly used up.

Harvey did not see how the liver could make so much blood so fast. He measured the amount of blood that the heart could hold, which was the most it could pump at each beat. He also counted the number of pulse beats in a minute. From these two figures, he calculated the amount of blood the heart could pump in a certain length of time. He stated that the figure he found was "a larger quantity . . . than is contained in the whole body!"[5]

Instead of making huge amounts of blood and using them up, Harvey believed that the body used a much smaller amount of blood over and over. This meant that blood had to move through the body in a circle. Instead of being used up, it had to return to the heart and be pumped out again.

The blood's circle through the body works

much like the smaller circle through the lungs, Harvey wrote. The left ventricle pushes blood into the aorta. From there the blood goes into smaller and smaller arteries throughout the body. As in the lungs, small arteries connect to small veins. (Again, Harvey did not know how this happened. We now know that capillaries do the job.) The small veins join larger ones, like streams joining a river. The blood in all the veins flows back to the heart. The blood enters the right atrium through the two venae cavae. (The upper vena cava brings blood from the upper part of the body. The lower vena cava carries blood from the lower part.) Then the blood goes to the right ventricle and out to the lungs.

Harvey used two main arguments to show that the blood has to move in circles. One argument relied on his measurements of the amount of blood pumped by the heart. Measuring things is a common part of science today, but in Harvey's time it was a new idea. Harvey was one of the first scientists to prove an idea by measurement.

The valves in the veins were Harvey's second proof of his idea. He had been thinking about these valves ever since Fabricius had shown them to him in Padua. Fabricius thought that the valves simply slowed the movement of blood and kept the blood from settling in the body's lower half. Harvey, however, noticed that Fabricius's "little doors" opened in just one direction. (Harvey wrote in his book that in dissections, he could not push a tool downward through the veins without destroying the valves. The tool could be pushed upward easily, however.) The valves let blood move only one way, from the body toward the heart.

Harvey showed more about the veins by tying a cloth fairly tightly around a man's upper arm. The veins in the lower arm swelled. On them, a few inches apart, Harvey saw little knots or lumps. These were the valves. After a moment the man's hand became darker than his other hand.

The veins in the arm are just under the skin, so the fairly tight cloth blocked blood flow into them. The arteries lie deeper inside the arm, so the cloth did not stop blood from flowing through them. As a result, blood flowed toward the man's hand but could not flow back. The extra blood made the veins swell and the hand become darker.

If Harvey tied the cloth very tightly, the veins did not swell. The arteries in the upper arm, above the cloth, swelled instead. The hand became pale instead of dark. This was because the cloth cut off blood flow in both arteries and veins. The hand became pale because of lack of blood. The arteries above the cloth filled with blood.

These experiments showed that blood flowed toward the hand in the arteries. It came back to the heart in the veins.

Another experiment also showed which way the blood flowed in the veins. It, too, used a cloth that blocked blood in the arm veins but not the arteries. After tying the cloth, Harvey pressed a finger on a swollen vein just above a valve. He moved another finger along the vein toward the heart, also pressing down. The vein between the two fingers seemed to disappear. This was because the moving finger pushed the blood out of the vein. The other finger kept more blood from flowing in. The vein above the next valve toward the heart stayed swollen. A finger pressing on it could not force blood into the empty part of the vein. If the finger at the lower end of the vein was removed, however, the whole vein swelled and darkened once again. This experiment showed that blood in the veins flows only toward the heart.

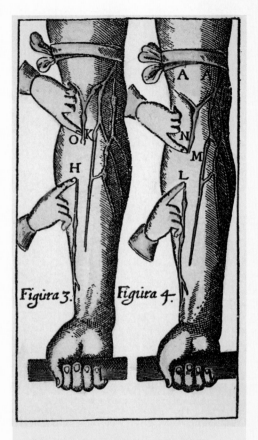

This illustration from Harvey's book shows veins in the arm. In the first picture, Harvey shows that pressing on part of the vein makes that part seem to disappear. The valve at O keeps the blood from flowing into the part of the vein between O and H, which has been emptied by the pressing fingers.

Chapter fourteen of Harvey's book had just one paragraph. It summed up what he had shown about the heart and circulation. It ended this way: "It is absolutely necessary to conclude that the blood in the animal body is impelled [pushed] in a circle, and is in a state of ceaseless motion; that this is the act or function which the heart performs by means of its pulse; and that is the . . . only end [purpose] of the motion and contraction of the heart."[6]

With these words, William Harvey announced a completely new way of thinking about how one of the most important parts of the body works.

4

Adventures at Home and Abroad

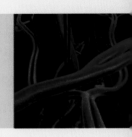

LATE IN HIS LIFE, WILLIAM HARVEY told John Aubrey that "after his book on the circulation of the blood came out . . . he fell mightily in his practice [lost many patients]. . . . 'Twas believed by the vulgar that he was crackbrained. . . . All the physicians were against his opinion and envied him; many wrote against him."[1]

Harvey may have been remembering things as worse than they were. Some doctors did write books disagreeing with his ideas. Some also said the ideas were not new. Other doctors, however, defended Harvey's work.

Harvey's real problem was that neither his attackers nor his defenders understood him. Most appear to have read his book carelessly.

They often stated his ideas incorrectly. They did not use experiments to disprove or support his claims. They agreed or disagreed with him depending on how his ideas fit with their own beliefs.

Most scientists just ignored Harvey's ideas. Anatomy teachers did not mention them. Doctors did not change their treatments because of them. It took twenty or thirty years for Harvey's discoveries to become well known. Considering how great a change in medical beliefs Harvey proposed, though, other scientists' acceptance of his views was really fairly rapid.

As for losing patients, it was true that Harvey stopped being the only doctor at St. Bartholomew's in 1632. An assistant did most of Harvey's work after that. Harvey spent less time at the Royal College, too. He resigned as treasurer there in 1629. This was not because doctors were angry about his ideas, though. It was because he now spent most of his time as a physician of King Charles. Harvey became one of the king's regular doctors in 1630.

Life at Court

Charles I was a handsome man. He was slender and, like Harvey, short. He spoke with a stammer. He was fond of fine clothes, and he loved to collect works of art. Like many rich Englishmen, he also enjoyed riding horses and hunting deer.

Charles had a more dignified court than his father. He insisted that people treat him like a king at all times. Only the queen could sit when he was in the room, for example. He believed that kings ruled by the will of God. Indeed, they were almost like gods on Earth and should always be obeyed. Kings before Charles also had felt this way, but people in Charles's time were starting to question these beliefs.

King Charles and Harvey became friends. Charles let Harvey dissect deer killed in hunts. Sometimes the king even helped in this work. Harvey, in turn, showed the king his latest

King Charles I was Harvey's patron and friend. Harvey, in turn, remained loyal to the king all his life.

discoveries, which Charles found very interesting. Harvey dedicated his book about the heart and blood partly to King Charles. He wrote:

> The heart of animals is the foundation of their life, the sovereign [ruler] of everything within them, the sun of their microcosm [tiny world], that upon which all growth depends, from which all power proceeds. The King, in like manner, is the foundation of his kingdom, the sun of the world around him, the heart of the republic, the fountain whence all power, all grace doth flow. . . . Accept therefore, . . . I most humbly beseech [beg] you, illustrious Prince, this, my new Treatise on the Heart; you, who are yourself the new light of this age, and indeed its very heart. . . .[2]

Harvey showed King Charles a living human heart once. Harvey heard about a young nobleman who had been hurt in a fall as a child. A large sore had formed on the boy's chest. The sore healed after a long time, but a hole remained. The boy grew into a healthy young man, but he wore a metal plate over the hole to protect it.

King Charles enjoyed learning about Harvey's discoveries. Here Harvey is explaining his ideas about blood circulation to the king and his son, who later became Charles II.

Harvey met the young man and saw the hole. He wrote that it was big enough to put three fingers and a thumb inside. He also saw "a certain fleshy part sticking out."[3] This moved constantly, and Harvey decided that it was the man's heart.

Harvey took the young man to see King Charles. The king held the man's heart in his hand. This did not hurt the young man, who said that he could not even feel it. The young man's strange situation showed Harvey that the heart was less fragile than most people thought. It also showed that the heart could not feel touch. This is true of most organs inside the body.

Harvey was popular at King Charles's court. Many noblemen as well as the king liked him and asked him to be their doctor. One of Harvey's noble patients was the Earl of Arundel, who often called him "honest little Harvey." The earl seemed to enjoy Harvey's energy. In a letter, he described him as "that little perpetual [constant] movement called Dr. Harvey."[4]

One time the Earl of Arundel met a very old farmer named Thomas Parr. People claimed that Parr was 152 years old. Arundel brought "Old Parr" to London to meet the king. Many people visited the amazing old man, bringing him rich foods and strong liquor. After a few months of this life, Parr became ill. He died on November 14, 1635. The earl asked Harvey to cut open the old man's body and examine it. Arundel wanted to know why Parr had died.

Harvey found that Parr had been, for the most part, a healthy old man. (He did not say whether he thought Parr was really as old as people claimed.) Parr had some heart problems that old people often have. Harvey did not think these killed him, though. He blamed Parr's death on "a sudden adoption of a mode [way] of living unnatural to him."[5]

Harvey wrote that Parr died from two things that still harm people: bad diet and air pollution. He pointed out that in the country, Parr had lived a healthy life. He got a lot of exercise and was happy. He did not eat or drink much. All that changed when Parr came to London. Harvey thought that unhealthy foods and alcohol had helped to make Parr sick.

The change of air, said Harvey, had harmed Parr even more: "All his life [Parr] had enjoyed absolutely clean . . . coolish and circulating air. . . . But life in London . . . lacks this advantage. . . . It is full of the filth of men, animals, canals and other forms of dirt. . . . In addition . . . there is the . . . grime from the smoke of . . . coal constantly used as fuel for fires. The air in London therefore is always heavy."[6] Harvey thought Old Parr had died of suffocation caused by the bad London air.

Harvey's conclusions came too late to save Parr. Sometimes, though, Harvey was able to use his medical knowledge to help people. For example, he saved the lives of some women who were accused of being witches in 1634. Most people of Harvey's time believed in witches. They thought that some people chose to be slaves of the devil. In return, the devil gave these people magic powers, and they became witches. They could use their powers to hurt or kill other people and animals. When country people had bad luck, they blamed witches. Old women were often accused of being witches. Many were tortured or killed.

In 1633, an eleven-year-old boy in

People of Harvey's time believed that witches had magic powers and could call up evil spirits. Harvey saved the lives of several women who were accused of being witches.

Lancashire (northwest England) told a strange tale. He said he had been kidnapped by a witch. The witch, a woman he knew, took him to a feast that many witches attended. The boy escaped, ran home, and told his father what had happened. Later the boy and his father related the tale to two judges. The boy named seventeen people he had seen at the feast. Later he added more names.

Almost thirty people were arrested because of what the boy said. The story of the "Lancashire witches" spread through England, and King Charles heard about it. Charles was not sure that he believed in witches, even though his father did.

People believed that all witches had a special lump or other mark somewhere on their bodies, put there by the devil. Judges at the Lancashire trial wanted doctors to look for such a mark on the accused people. This was often done in witchcraft trials. King Charles sent Harvey to be one of the doctors.

Harvey and other doctors examined four of

the accused women. Harvey found "nothing unnatural" on them. Because of his report, the king freed the women. The Lancashire boy was then questioned again. He finally admitted that he and his father made up the whole story. When the judges heard that, they released the other accused people.

Travels in Europe

Harvey sometimes traveled with the king or other members of the court. They liked to have an experienced doctor with them on long journeys. Harvey saw these trips as fine chances to learn about the plants and animals of distant places.

Harvey made his longest trip in 1636, when he went with the Earl of Arundel and others on a diplomatic mission to Germany. At that time, much of Europe was in ruins because of a long war. It was later called the Thirty Years' War.

Harvey had already seen the war's effects during a trip to France six years before. At that time, he described the terrible scene in a letter to a friend. The letter showed his pity for the miserable people he saw. It also showed his urge to study living things, no matter where he was. Harvey wrote: "I can only complain that . . . we could scarce[ly] see a dog, crow, . . . or any bird . . . to anatomize [dissect]. . . . Some few miserable people, the relics of the war and the plague, . . . a famine had made anatomies [skeletons] before I came. It is scarce[ly] credible [believable] in so rich, populous and plentiful countries as these were that so much misery . . . should in so short a time be as we have seen."[7]

When Harvey returned to Europe in 1636 with the Earl of Arundel, the Thirty Years' War was still going on. Conditions were just as bad as before. Arundel's group saw some people so starved that they could hardly crawl. Hunger had turned healthier people into thieves. The earl's party gave the hungry people all the food they could spare. Still, as the group traveled up the Rhine River, they often slept on their boats to protect themselves from attack.

Harvey went into the woods to look at plants,

1636

This map shows the countries of Europe as they were at the time of Harvey's trip in 1636. Much of Europe was in ruins at the time because of the Thirty Years' War.

animals, and rocks whenever he could. He sometimes stayed so long that Arundel thought he must be lost. When Harvey finally returned, the earl scolded him. He reminded Harvey that both thieves and dangerous animals lived in the woods and that either could have attacked him.

Harvey left Arundel's group for a while to do an errand for King Charles. The king had asked him to buy some paintings in Italy. Before Harvey could do so, however, he ran into trouble.

Plague had been sweeping through Italy. This deadly disease spreads from person to person. Harvey had a paper that said he did not have plague. Still, officials in Treviso, a town near Venice, decided that his paper was not good enough. They feared he might carry the disease. They would not let him enter the town or go on with his journey.

The officials told Harvey to go to Treviso's hospital, but he said no. He was afraid he would become sick if he went there. In that case, the officials said, he would have to sleep in the fields outside of town.

After a few days of this, Harvey was furious. His back hurt. He could not get anyone to listen to him. He sent a series of angry letters to Lord Denbigh, another noble friend, in Venice. He asked Lord Denbigh to make the people at Treviso let him go. "I never longed for anything in all my life so much as . . . to be gone from this place," Harvey wrote.[8]

Denbigh was able to help only a little. Harvey had to spend three miserable weeks in Treviso before the officials let him go. He had little luck in buying pictures after his release. (He did, however, make some enjoyable visits to hospitals and medical schools in Italy.) No doubt he was glad to rejoin Arundel and start back to England. Still, he was bound to remember this nine-month trip through Europe as one of the greatest adventures of his life.

5

Civil War

WHILE WILLIAM HARVEY LOOKED AT THE ruin brought by war abroad, the storm clouds of a different war were beginning to gather at home. This threat of war grew out of disagreements between King Charles and Parliament.

War Clouds Gather

In Harvey's time, members of Parliament were elected by the nobles and by men who owned land. (Today, any adult citizen of Britain can vote.) British rulers in those days had far more power than they have now. They could choose when to let Parliament meet, for example. However, Parliament had power as well. It decided what taxes could be imposed and how the money should be spent. It also was supposed to approve laws made by the ruler's ministers.

King Charles thought he did not need Parliament. He did not let it meet between 1629 and 1640. He ordered a new tax without its approval. This angered many people, who felt that their representatives should have a voice in the country's government.

Religion was part of the quarrel, too. In 1534, under King Henry VIII, England had broken away from the Catholic Church. The country had formed its own Protestant Church, the Church of England. Many British Protestants hated and feared Catholicism. Charles's wife, Henrietta Maria, was a Catholic. Charles made changes in the Church of England that many people feared might lead it back to Catholicism.

Some people wanted to do more than reverse Charles's changes in the Church. They wanted to make changes in the opposite direction. They planned to remove certain ceremonies that they thought were too much like "popery." They also wanted everyone to live a more strict and moral life. They hoped to outlaw theaters and dancing, for example. These people were called Puritans. The Puritans opposed King Charles's religious changes even more strongly than other Protestants did.

Most people in Scotland were strongly Protestant. They refused to accept the king's religious changes. When the king insisted, the Scots gathered an army. Charles needed money to pay an English army to fight them. To get the money, he had to call a meeting of Parliament.

Parliament said it would give the king nothing until he agreed to its demands. At last, King Charles gave in. He agreed to some reforms in the Church. He dropped his new tax. He signed a law saying that Parliament had to be called at least once every three years and agreed not to dismiss it without its permission. Parliament took full advantage of this last change. It stayed in session for the next thirteen years. No wonder that sitting was called the Long Parliament!

These changes were not enough for

Parliament, however. In November 1641, it gave King Charles a long list of complaints. The list included everything Parliament thought the king had done wrong since the start of his reign. Some historians think Thomas Jefferson used this document as a model for his Declaration of Independence.

King Charles was very angry about Parliament's actions. He tried to arrest five Parliament leaders for treason. (Treason is rebellion against a country's government.) He failed, and his action made Parliament's resentment worse. More and more people came to believe that only war could settle the question of whether the king or Parliament would rule Britain. As one member of Parliament said, "We have . . . slid into this beginning of a civil war, by one . . . accident after another, as waves of the sea."[1]

William Harvey had become one of King Charles's chief doctors in 1639. He now spent most of his time as part of the king's court. He lived at Whitehall, the king's London palace. No one knows what Harvey thought of Parliament or religion, but he clearly felt very loyal to the king, his friend. Harvey would show his loyalty in many ways during the dark days to come.

A Country Torn Apart

King Charles and his family fled London shortly after his failed attempt to arrest the Parliament leaders. A little later, Harvey joined him. The little doctor probably was with Charles when the king raised his personal flag at a small town named Nottingham on August 22, 1642. There King Charles called for supporters to help him fight Parliament. Both sides gathered armies. The civil war had begun.

Harvey told John Aubrey he was with the king at the Battle of Edgehill. This battle, the first major fight of the war, took place on October 22, 1642. Two of the king's children were also there. One was the twelve-year-old Prince of Wales, the heir to the throne. The other was the nine-year-old Duke of York. King

This map shows England at the time of the civil war between the forces of King Charles I and Parliament. William Harvey remained loyal to the king during the war and was with the king at the Battle of Edgehill.

Charles told Harvey to protect the boys during the battle.

In the morning, before the fighting started, Harvey sat with the children under a bush. The soldiers were a short distance away. When the cannons began to fire, Harvey calmly took out a book and read to the boys. A cannonball, however, soon landed much too close for comfort. The little group hastily moved out of range.

Both sides claimed victory at Edgehill. No one knew what would happen next. Slowly the country began to prepare for more fighting.

Most of the people in London supported Parliament. They thought the king might attack the city. Some began to form a rough army. Others roamed as mobs through the streets.

One mob attacked the deserted living quarters around the king's palace and broke into many rooms, including Harvey's. The mob stole or smashed most of his possessions. Worse still, they destroyed his notes and papers, which recorded the results of many years of scientific work. For example, he lost all the notes for a book he was planning to write about insects. Harvey later told John Aubrey that the loss of his papers was the worst thing that had ever happened to him.

Soon after the Battle of Edgehill, King Charles went to Oxford. Most people in that city supported him. The king lived in Oxford for the next three and a half years, and Harvey stayed there with him.

The king's choice of headquarters surely pleased Harvey. Oxford is home to one of England's greatest universities. Harvey thus had plenty of other educated people with whom to talk while living there. He could even do a little

Merton College is part of Oxford, one of England's greatest universities. Harvey stayed in Oxford with King Charles during the civil war and was warden of Merton for several years.

scientific work. One Oxford professor had a hen, and Harvey often examined its eggs. He was gathering information for another book, which would describe the way animals develop before birth.

Harvey had a new job during his years at Oxford. The warden of Merton College had left to join the Parliament forces. Merton is one of the colleges that make up Oxford University. At the king's urging, the college gave the warden's job to Harvey in April 1645. The post gave the aging Harvey a place to live. It was also somewhat fitting because many Merton College graduates became doctors. Whatever the warden's duties might have been, however, Harvey had little chance to carry them out in those unsettled times.

At first, the king's side appeared to be winning the war. Then, however, Parliament improved its army. One of the new army's leaders was named Oliver Cromwell. Cromwell, a member of Parliament, was a stern man who shared many of the Puritans' beliefs.

Under Cromwell's leadership, the Parliament army began to defeat King Charles's forces. On April 27, 1646, after troops had besieged Oxford for almost a year, the king fled the city in disguise. Harvey stayed behind.

King Charles gave himself up on May 5, 1646. (His wife and the Prince of Wales, however, escaped overseas.) Cromwell and the other Parliament leaders kept him a prisoner for several years. As far as is known, Harvey saw his friend for the last time late in 1646.

In 1647, King Charles escaped briefly, and new fighting broke out. Parliament then decided that the king was too dangerous to live. It put King Charles on trial for treason. The Parliament's court found Charles guilty of making war on his own people. The king was beheaded on January 30, 1649.

Parliament announced that Britain would no longer be ruled by kings and queens. It set up a republican government called the Commonwealth. But in 1653, with the army's help, Oliver Cromwell in effect took control of the country. He ruled Britain almost as a dictator until he died in 1658.

By then the British people were tired of Cromwell's government. They hated its high taxes and strict laws. In 1660, they brought Charles I's son back from overseas and asked

Oliver Cromwell led the Parliament armies to victory over King Charles. Cromwell ruled England during the last years of Harvey's life. Cromwell's statue stands in St. Ives, Cambridgeshire, where he was a farmer.

him to rule the country. Parliament kept the most important rights it had gained, however.

The boy whom Harvey had protected during the Battle of Edgehill was thirty years old by then. He became Charles II. He shared his father's interest in science. He no doubt remembered the little doctor he had seen in his childhood, but he returned to power too late to help William Harvey.

6

Reproduction of Animals

WILLIAM HARVEY WAS SIXTY-EIGHT years old in 1646, when Oxford surrendered to Parliament. By then he had every right to be a sad and bitter man. He had lost his patron and friend, King Charles. He had lost his job as court physician. The new government made him pay a heavy fine for supporting the king. His home and goods were destroyed. Worse still, so were most records of his scientific work. His wife was soon to die as well.

Harvey was not entirely alone, however. He still had his brothers. Thomas Harvey, William's father, had told his seven sons to "unite with one another fast knit together," and they had always done just that.[1] Five of the seven became rich merchants who traded with Turkey and other

Harvey's brother Eliab (above), gave Harvey a place to live after Harvey lost his home and possessions in the civil war.

countries in the East. Three had died of illness during the war years, and some left William large sums of money. Now Eliab and Daniel, the two brothers left, gave William a home. He spent the rest of his life in his brothers' houses near London. John Aubrey said that Eliab also managed William's money.

More About the Heart and Blood

William Harvey buried his sadness in work. For the first time, he published a reply to a critic of his book about the heart and blood. Since the time the book had been published, Harvey wrote, "there has . . . been scarcely a day . . . in which I have not heard both good and ill report of the circulation which I discovered."[2] Still, for twenty years he had not bothered to answer his critics in print. He once told friends: "It is not weighty enough for me to trouble the Republic of Letters [that is, to write]. . . . Perish [let die] my thoughts if they are empty and my experiments if they are wrong. . . . If I am right, sometime, in the end the human race will not disdain the truth."[3]

The criticism Harvey answered came from Jean Riolan, a famous French doctor. In 1648, Riolan published a book that claimed to disprove some of Harvey's ideas. Most of

Riolan's thinking was muddled. For instance, he claimed that Harvey was right about circulation in the large blood vessels. Then, however, he said that the blood in smaller blood vessels moved in the opposite direction.

Harvey wrote two long letters to Riolan and published them as a small book in 1649. In this booklet, Harvey answered all of Riolan's objections. He also offered new evidence that supported his own ideas.

One question Harvey answered was about the colors of the blood. Blood in arteries is bright red, but blood in veins looks almost black. This appears to suggest that there are two kinds of blood. If that was true, Riolan said, Harvey's ideas about blood circulation would have to be wrong.

Harvey told Riolan he had put blood from an artery in one bowl and blood from a vein in another. He let the blood thicken or clot. Both clots, Harvey said, were the same color. (Today we know why blood has different colors. The coloring matter in blood is bright red when it carries oxygen. After this substance loses its oxygen in the body, it turns dark.)

Riolan was one of the last to object to Harvey's views. By the late 1640s, most doctors agreed that Harvey was right. At about the same time he made his answer to Riolan, Harvey wrote, "I perceive that the wonderful circulation of the blood, first found out by me, is consented to by almost all."[4] John Aubrey wrote that Harvey's ideas were "at last, in about 20 or 30 years' time, . . . received in all the universities of the world."[5]

How Animals Develop

In 1651, Harvey published his second major book. It was called *Essays on the Generation* [Reproduction] *of Animals*. It described how animals' lives begin and showed how they develop before birth. Harvey had been working on this book for many years. He probably wrote much of it during the slow days at Oxford or even before.

At first, Harvey did not plan to publish this

Guliclmus Harveu.
de
Generatione Animalium.

The title page of Harvey's book about the reproduction and development of animals shows the Roman god Jupiter. Jupiter is releasing animals from an egg.

book. A friend, Dr. George Ent, made him change his mind. Ent visited Harvey around Christmas in 1648. Harvey was again doing scientific work, and at first the old man appeared calm and cheerful. Then, however, Ent asked whether all was well with him, and Harvey replied: "How can it be, while the commonwealth [country] is full of distractions, and I myself am still in the open sea? . . . Truly, did I not find solace [comfort] in my studies . . . I should feel little desire for longer life."[6]

Harvey mentioned that he had written a long book on animal reproduction and development. Ent was amazed that "so vast a treasure had remained so long concealed."[7] He urged Harvey to let him print it. He no doubt hoped the project would cheer up his old friend.

At first Harvey objected. He was tired and in ill health, and he no longer enjoyed arguing about scientific ideas. In the end, however, Harvey agreed to let Ent publish the book.

Harvey's book on animals was much longer than the one on the heart. Like his lecture notes, it mentioned many things he had seen during his life. It had seventy-two "exercises," or short chapters.

The first part of Harvey's book described the development of the chick in the hen's egg. Harvey's old teacher, Fabricius, had written a similar description. Fabricius had pointed out a "little scar" on the inside of the egg. He thought it was not important, but Harvey realized that it is very important indeed. It is the place where the chick begins developing. Harvey said this spot "expands like the pupil of the eye" as the chick starts to grow.[8]

Late on the third day of development, Harvey said, the "leaping point" appears. This tiny spot is the first part of the chick that moves. At first Harvey could see this spot only in bright light with a magnifying glass. When the point swelled, it looked "like the smallest spark of fire."[9] When it contracted, it almost disappeared.

The spot is the color of blood, and Harvey believed that it was blood. He thought it was proof that blood appeared before the heart

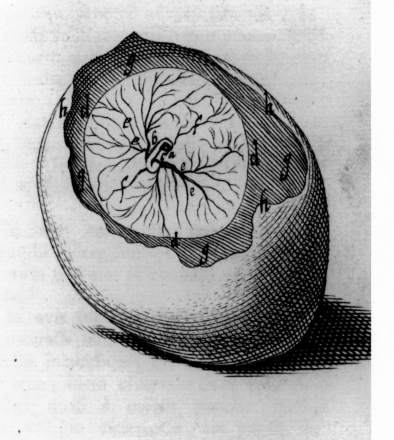

This illustration shows an unborn chick developing inside an egg. Harvey made important discoveries about how chickens and other animals develop before birth.

was formed. Later scientists with microscopes showed, however, that this spot is in fact the chick's heart. Harvey could not see the heart's shape while it was so small. Soon after Harvey's death, another scientist proved that the heart becomes active before blood appears. For the most part though, Harvey's account of chick development was accurate.

Harvey compared the unborn chick's development with that of the deer. He had been able to dissect many deer because King Charles liked to hunt them. For this reason, he chose deer as an example of animals that give birth to living young rather than lay eggs. It was not a wise choice, though, because unborn deer develop somewhat differently from most other mammals.

How Life Begins

In the second part of his book, Harvey tried to guess what happens at the very start of a new life. He knew that a male and a female have to mate before a new animal can be produced. But what does each parent contribute? This had been a mystery to early scientists, and it remained a mystery to Harvey.

Again, Harvey's problem was that he did not use a microscope. When a male and a female animal mate, the male sends out cells called sperm. They look something like tadpoles. They can swim very fast. If one of the sperm cells enters an egg cell made by the female, a new life begins. Sperm and egg cells are too tiny to see with just a magnifying glass. They were discovered many years after Harvey's death.

Harvey thought unborn animals develop one part at a time. In other words, some parts are made before others. Fabricius had thought this, too. After scientists discovered sperm cells, though, many came to believe that each of these cells held the complete form of a new animal. They even drew pictures showing "little men" inside human sperm cells. Other scientists thought the whole design of the baby was in the egg. Both groups thought a new animal developed just by growing larger, without changing shape or adding parts. This idea was not disproved until 1825. Scientists now know that Harvey and his teachers were right. A new animal takes form as it grows.

Harvey added three essays on human pregnancy and birth to his book. In these essays, he described things he had seen as a doctor. He gave good advice to doctors and nurses who help women give birth. This part of his book was used as a textbook for many years.

Harvey's book about animal reproduction did not stir up the arguments that his book on the heart had. It has not remained as famous, either. It contained only one new discovery, the finding that the "little scar" marked the beginning of the unborn chick. The book contained some brilliant guesses that Harvey could not prove. It also had some important mistakes. After scientists with microscopes corrected these mistakes, Harvey's second book was almost forgotten.

Last Days

IN 1651, A YOUNG MAN NAMED JOHN Aubrey came to William Harvey for advice. Aubrey was a cousin of one of Harvey's patients. He was twenty-five at the time, and Harvey was seventy-three. Aubrey was about to make a trip to Italy. Harvey told him "what company to keep, what books to read, [and] how to manage my studies."[1]

Then and later, Aubrey found Harvey "willing to instruct any that were modest [and] respectful to him."[2] Aubrey included a chapter on Harvey in a book he wrote about famous people's lives titled *Brief Lives*. Historians think that some of Aubrey's statements may not be correct. Still, Aubrey is one of the few writers who knew Harvey well whose words have survived. Much of what we know about Harvey's personality comes from Aubrey's sketch. Aubrey said he learned most of his information by talking with the doctor himself.

Talks with a Young Friend

Aubrey decided he liked the white-haired doctor. Harvey was not "stiff, proud, starched . . . as other formal doctors are."[3] The two became friends and talked for hours at a time.

Harvey told Aubrey his opinions on many subjects. Aubrey said Harvey was a fair-minded man, "far from bigotry."[4] Harvey's language could be blunt at times, however. He once told Aubrey that "man was but [just] a great mischievous baboon [a kind of monkey]."[5]

As an old man, Harvey suffered from a disease called gout. Gout is a kind of arthritis. It causes great pain in the joints. If sore joints woke him up at night, Harvey told Aubrey, he went up to a porch on the roof of his brother's house. He sat outside with his legs bared to the frosty air. Sometimes he even soaked his aching feet in a

When Harvey was an old man, his hair, once "black as a raven," became gray. But his interest in science was as great as ever.

bucket of cold water. He kept them there "till he was almost dead with cold."[6] Then he went inside and sat by the stove to warm up. The intense cold made the pain go away.

Harvey apparently woke up at night often. His busy mind would not let him sleep. When Harvey was wakeful at night, he paced around his room until he grew cold enough to shiver. Then he went back to bed and slept "very comfortably."[7] He told Aubrey that he thought best in the dark and even "delight[ed] to be in the dark" during the daytime.[8] At one of his brothers' country houses, he had caves dug in the earth. He liked to sit in these cool caves in the summer and think.

Harvey as an Old Man

Harvey's mind remained lively and busy to the end of his life. He studied mathematics. He wrote long letters to friends and fellow scientists. He still treated a few patients, too. Most were old friends who wanted no other doctor.

Harvey no longer spent much time at the

Royal College of Physicians. For one thing, he had to get government permission for each visit to London. The new government did not trust him because he had helped King Charles in the civil war. He did not forget his friends in the capital, however. He gave money to the Royal College so it could build a new library and museum. The library, which contained a statue of Harvey, opened in 1654. Sad to say, the library burned down in a great fire that swept through London in 1666.

Harvey wrote to a friend in April 1657, "I am not only ripe in years, but also—let me admit—a little weary. It seems to me indeed that I am entitled to ask for an honorable discharge [from life]."[9] Fate, it seems, agreed. A little over a month later, at ten o'clock in the morning, Harvey found he could not speak. He had what doctors of the time called the "dead palsy" in his tongue. Most likely he had had a stroke. Blood to part of his brain was cut off, which left him partly paralyzed. He died later that day, June 3, 1657. He was seventy-nine years old.

Harvey was buried in the family's vault at Hempstead, in Essex. Aubrey went to his funeral on June 25 and helped to carry Harvey into the vault. Most members of the Royal College were there, too, dressed in their academic gowns.

In 1883, Harvey was reburied in a large tomb in the Hempstead church. The tomb, and a sculpture of Harvey, can still be seen there. Scientists of his time called Harvey "immortal," and so he is. Thanks to his brilliant work, his name has never died.

A New Kind of Science

ONE WRITER SAID WILLIAM HARVEY'S "sharpness of wit and brightness of mind, as a light darted from heaven, has illuminated the whole learned world."[1] Harvey's was one of several great minds who brought new light to seventeenth-century science.

The Italian scientist Galileo was another. Galileo used the newly invented telescope to see other planets. He helped prove that the sun, not the earth, was the center of our solar system. Most people before him thought the earth was the center. Harvey may have even met Galileo at Padua.

Learning from Nature

A group of British scientists formed the Royal Society of London in 1660. Charles II supported it, just as his father, Charles I, had helped Harvey. Isaac Newton was one member. He discovered the law of gravity. Antonie van Leeuwenhoek sent reports to the Royal Society from the Netherlands. He was the first to see germs (microorganisms) and sperm cells with a microscope. These men, too, helped to change science in the seventeenth century.

Men like these knew they were changing the way science worked. One scientist wrote in 1664, "I see how all the old rubbish [of outdated beliefs] must be thrown away, and the rotten buildings be overthrown . . . with so powerful an inundation [flood]" of new ideas.[2] These new scientists believed what they saw with their own eyes, not what they learned from books. "Nature herself must be our advisor," Harvey wrote.[3]

Scientists of Harvey's time began to test their ideas with experiments. In experiments, scientists change one small part of nature on purpose. They then see what else changes as a result. For instance, Harvey tied a cloth around his arm. This blocked blood flow in the veins below the cloth. Then Harvey looked for changes in those veins. When he did these things, he was performing an experiment. The experiment helped him learn which way blood flowed in the veins. In 1656 Harvey told the Royal College of Physicians to "search out and study the secret of nature by . . . experiment."[4]

Most experiments involve measuring something. Harvey measured when he tried to find out how much blood the heart could pump. Scientists today learn mostly through observing, doing experiments, and measuring.

Opening a New Field

By the time of Harvey's death, most anatomists had accepted his ideas about the heart and blood. Later in the century, they built on those ideas to make new discoveries. Marcello Malpighi, an Italian scientist (born in the same year Harvey's book on the heart was published), found capillaries in a frog's lungs with a microscope in 1660. These were the "missing link" between arteries and veins that Harvey

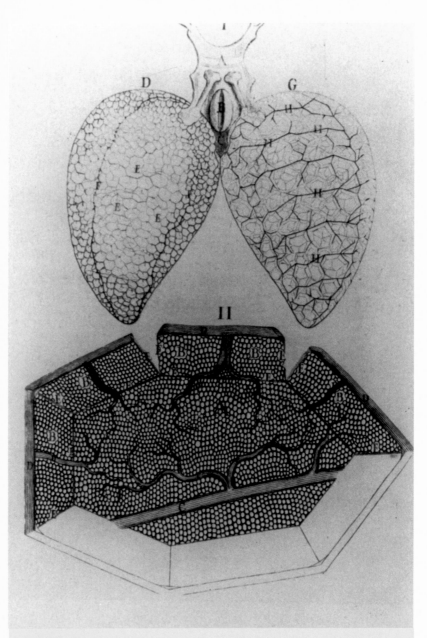

Harvey did not know how blood moved from the arteries to the veins. An Italian scientist named Marcello Malpighi found the answer in 1660, three years after Harvey's death. Using a microscope, Malpighi found tiny vessels called capillaries that connected arteries and veins. This picture shows capillaries in the lung of a frog.

could not see. Other scientists improved Harvey's way of measuring the amount of blood the heart pumped with each beat.

It took longer for Harvey's ideas to change medicine. At first, doctors did not see how his findings could help sick people. New discoveries had to be added to Harvey's work before it could be used in this way. For example, the stethoscope was invented in 1816. This tool was first used to listen to sounds from the lungs, but it also lets doctors hear sounds that the heart makes. They learned that sick hearts make different sounds from healthy ones. Doctors use these sounds to identify some kinds of heart disease.

Near the end of his book about the heart, William Harvey wrote that his discovery opened "a field of such vast extent . . . that . . . my whole life . . . would not suffice [be enough] for its completion."[5] Scientists are still exploring this field, which is called cardiology. (*Card-* or *cord-* is a Latin word root meaning *heart*. Harvey used a form of this root, *Cordis*, in the title of his book.) They have learned how to make sick hearts

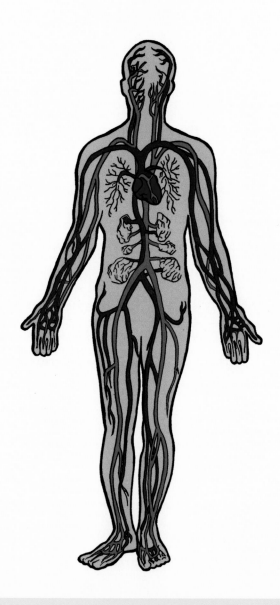

This drawing shows the circulation of blood as doctors understand it today. William Harvey was the first to prove that blood moved in circles.

healthier with medicines. They have learned to repair damaged hearts with surgery. All these advances are, in a way, based on Harvey's work. Each time a doctor or nurse feels a pulse, listens to heart sounds with a stethoscope, or measures blood pressure, he or she draws on knowledge that came from William Harvey.

But Harvey's importance goes even beyond this. He was one of the first scientists to show how the body works—a subject of study named physiology. He was one of the first to compare human and animal bodies. He was one of the first to use what is now called the scientific method. For all these reasons, William Harvey is truly an immortal figure in science.

Afterword:
Helping the Heart

Some people's hearts are not strong enough to pump blood through their bodies. They may have been born with a heart problem, or they may have developed heart trouble as they grew older.

In William Harvey's time, no one could have helped these people. Today, though, new devices may save their lives. Some devices tell the heart how fast to beat. Others take over the pumping job of the ventricles.

Pacemakers

Long after Harvey's day, scientists learned that an electric current controls the heart. The current comes from the pacemaker, a group of cells in the right atrium. Pulses in this current set the speed of the heartbeat. The pacemaker sends out pulses more often when a person exercises, for instance. That makes the heart beat faster. Blood then flows more quickly, bringing the body the extra oxygen it needs.

Some people's pacemakers do not send their electric pulses at the right speed. In others, nerve blocks keep the pulses from reaching the ventricles. An artificial pacemaker can solve these problems. This device sends out pulses of electricity, just as a person's own pacemaker would.

A Canadian engineer made the first artificial pacemaker in 1950. Swedish inventors made better ones in the late 1950s. Unlike the first device, these could be left in the body. They were about the size of a hockey puck. Making use of miniaturized electronics, today's pacemakers can be as small as 2.54 cm (one inch) across.

The pacemaker's current comes from a generator. The generator contains a battery. It also includes a computer chip that sets the speed of the current's pulses. The outer case of the generator is made of titanium. This metal is very strong and does not harm the body.

In modern pacemakers, surgeons place the

generator just under the fat and skin of the chest wall. This is an easy operation. The patient can be awake while it is done. Batteries in early generators had to be replaced every two years, requiring a new operation each time. Such replacement is not needed any longer.

Wires go from the generator to the surface of the heart. They carry the pacemaker's current to the heart cells. They also send information about the heartbeat to the chip in the generator. At first, surgeons had to open a person's chest to attach the wires. Today, though, the wires can be threaded through a vein.

Some pacemakers control only the ventricles. Others send current to the atria as well. These are called dual [two]-chamber pacemakers. They cost more than the ones that affect just the ventricles, but they work better for many people. The best pacemakers can sense a person's activity level and change the speed of the heart to match it, just as the natural pacemaker does.

LVADs

Each year, about 400,000 people in the United States develop a disease called congestive heart failure. Their hearts become larger and weaker than they should be. These weak hearts cannot pump blood very well. People with this disease may feel tired and out of breath even when they are not exercising. Medicine helps some of these people. Others need a new heart.

Some people agree to donate their hearts or other organs if the they die suddenly. The organs can be transplanted into people whose own organs have failed. There are not enough donor hearts for all who need them, though. Some people must wait a long time for a new heart. Others are too sick to withstand the transplant operation, even if a heart could be found.

A device called an LVAD (left ventricular assist device) can help some people with this disease. The LVAD is a kind of pump. One common type of LVAD is a round device about

10 cm (4 inches) across. Surgeons place it under the muscles of the abdomen.

An LVAD can give a sick person's heart a rest and help the heart grow stronger. Then, sometimes, an operation can cut back the size of the swollen heart and improve the person's health. An LVAD also helps to keep a person alive until a transplant can be found. Some kinds of LVADs let people too sick for transplants live longer than they would with drugs alone.

William Harvey no doubt would have been very surprised to learn about pacemakers and LVADs. He would have been glad to know, though, that his discoveries about the heart had helped to make these lifesaving inventions possible.

Activities

Like William Harvey, you can do experiments to learn about the heart and the way blood moves through the body.

Heartbeat and Exercise
Materials needed:

- watch or clock that can measure seconds

Procedure:

Feel your wrist until you find your heartbeat or pulse. Count how many times your heart beats in one minute. Then run or do other heavy exercise for five or ten minutes. Now, count again the number of times your heart beats in one minute.

Questions:

How does exercise change the number of heartbeats in a minute? Why do you think the number changes in this way?

Anatomy of the Heart

Materials needed:

- get adult help, supervision, and permission
- two sheets drawing paper
- colored pencils or crayons
- knife
- heart of an animal (Get this from a butcher or a grocery-store meat department. A beef heart is best because it is big, but you can also use a turkey or a chicken heart.)

NOTE: Do not attempt the following activities without adult approval and supervision.

Procedure:

Look first at the outside of the heart. Draw a picture of the heart and the blood vessels you see. Then carefully cut open the heart. Draw another picture showing the inside of the heart. Label the different parts. Add arrows showing how you think the blood moves.

Questions:

Does this heart have the same number of chambers as a human heart? Can you see the valves in the heart? What blood vessels can you identify?

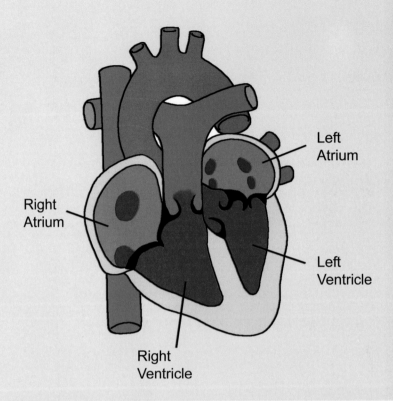

Right
Atrium

Left
Atrium

Left
Ventricle

Right
Ventricle

Working with an adult, cut open an animal heart from the butcher. Draw what you see. Is it like what William Harvey described?

_____

Veins and Movement of the Blood

Materials needed:

- piece of thread or thin string about a foot long

Procedure:

Wind the thread or string tightly around the base of your finger several times. Wait 30 seconds or a minute. *(Do not leave the thread on for longer than a minute!)* Then take the thread off.

Questions:

How does the feeling in your finger change after the thread has been wound around it for a minute? How does the finger's color change? Does the finger become warmer or colder than your other fingers? What do you think makes these changes happen?

Chronology

1578—William Harvey is born on April 1 in Folkestone, England.

1593—Begins studies at Cambridge University.

1597—Receives a B.A. from Cambridge.

1600—Begins medical studies at University of Padua in Italy.

1602—Receives Doctor of Medicine degree from University of Padua and M.D. degree from Cambridge.

1604—Receives license to practice medicine from Royal College of Physicians in London; marries Elizabeth Browne.

1609—Becomes physician of St. Bartholomew's Hospital in London.

1616—Begins giving Lumleian Lectures on anatomy at Royal College.

1618—Becomes a consulting doctor to King James I.

1625—Reports to Parliament about King James's death.

1628—Publishes book on the movement of the heart and blood.

1630—Becomes one of King Charles I's regular doctors.

1636—Travels to Germany with the Earl of Arundel.

1639—Becomes one of King Charles's chief doctors.

1642—English Civil War begins; Harvey is with King Charles at the Battle of Edgehill.

1645—Becomes warden of Merton College, Oxford; King Charles's army is defeated at the Battle of Naseby.

1646—King Charles surrenders to Parliament army.

1648—Publishes reply to critic of his ideas about blood circulation.

1649—King Charles is beheaded.

1651—Publishes a book on the generation (reproduction) of animals.

1652—Dies of a stroke on June 3.

Chapter Notes

Chapter 1. Learning to Be a Doctor

1. Thomas Fuller, quoted in Geoffrey Keynes, *The Life of William Harvey* (Oxford: Clarendon Press, 1966), p. 5.

2. Dr. Lever, Master of St. Johns, quoted in Keynes, p. 19.

3. Philip Cane, *Giants of Science* (New York: Pyramid Publications, 1961), p. 32.

4. Keynes, pp. 32–33.

Chapter 2. Harvey the Physician

1. Kenneth D. Keele, *William Harvey: The Man, the Physician, and the Scientist* (London: Nelson, 1965), p. 65.

2. John Aubrey, quoted in Geoffrey Keynes, *The Life of William Harvey* (Oxford: Clarendon Press, 1966), p. 434.

3. John Aubrey, quoted in Keynes, p. 437.

4. Keynes, p. 45.

5. William Harvey, *Prelectiones* (lecture notes), quoted in Keynes, p. 91.

6. Maurice Ashley, *Life in Stuart England* (New York: Putnam, 1964), p. 53.

7. Keynes, p. 386.

8. Sir Theodore de Mayerne, quoted in Keynes, p. 142.

Chapter 3. Movement of the Heart and Blood

1. William Harvey, *An Anatomical Essay on the Motion of the Heart and Blood in Animals*, translated by Robert Willis and revised by Alexander Bowie, in *The Harvard Classics*, Vol. 38: *Scientific Papers* (New York: Collier, 1910), p. 79.

2. Ibid., p. 79.

3. Ibid., p. 76.

4. Ibid., p. 106.

5. Ibid., p. 109.

6. Ibid., p. 129.

Chapter 4. Adventures at Home and Abroad

1. John Aubrey, quoted in Geoffrey Keynes, *The Life of William Harvey* (Oxford: Clarendon Press, 1966), p. 435.

2. William Harvey, *An Anatomical Essay on the Motion of the Heart and Blood in Animals*, translated by Robert Willis and revised by Alexander Bowie, in *The Harvard Classics*, Vol. 38: *Scientific Papers* (New York: Collier, 1910), p. 7x.

3. William Harvey, quoted in Keynes, p. 156.

4. Keynes, p. 257.

5. Ibid., p. 224.

6. Ibid.

7. Ibid., p. 194.

8. Ibid., p. 255.

Chapter 5. Civil War

1. Austin Woolrych, *Battles of the English Civil War* (New York: Macmillan, 1961), p. 34.

Chapter 6. Reproduction of Animals

1.Thomas Harvey's will, quoted in Geoffrey Keynes, *The Life of William Harvey* (Oxford: Clarendon Press, 1966), p. 129.

2. Keynes, p. 325.

3. Ibid., p. 322.

4. Ibid.

5. John Aubrey, quoted in Keynes, p. 435.

6. George Ent, quoted in Keynes, p. 330.

7. Keynes, p. 332.

8. William Harvey, *De Generatione Animalium*, quoted in Kenneth D. Keele, *William Harvey: The Man, the Physician, and the Scientist* (London: Nelson, 1965), p. 184.

9. William Harvey, *De Generatione Animalium*, quoted in Keele, p. 185.

Chapter 7. Last Days

1. John Aubrey, quoted in Geoffrey Keynes, *The Life of William Harvey* (Oxford: Clarendon Press, 1966), p. 434.

2. Ibid.

3. John Aubrey, quoted in Keynes, p. 437.

4. Ibid., p. 433.

5. Ibid.

6. Ibid., p. 435.

7. Ibid.

8. Ibid., p. 433.

9. Sherwin B. Nuland, *Doctors* (New York: Random House/Vintage, 1989), p. 143.

Chapter 8. A New Kind of Science

1. Dr. Samuel Garth, quoted in Geoffrey Keynes, *The Life of William Harvey* (Oxford: Clarendon Press, 1966), p. 423.

2. Henry Power, quoted in Sherwin B. Nuland, *Doctors* (New York: Random House/Vintage, 1989), p. 136.

3. Nuland, p. 143.

4. Keynes, p. 404.

5. William Harvey, *An Anatomical Essay on the Motion of the Heart and Blood in Animals*, translated by Robert Willis and revised by Alexander Bowie, in *The Harvard Classics*, Vol. 38: *Scientific Papers* (New York: Collier, 1910), p. 136.

Glossary

anatomy—The scientific study of the structure of living things.

aorta—The large artery that leads from the left ventricle of the heart to the body. It is the body's largest artery.

apothecary—A person who prepares and sells medicines, today known as a pharmacist.

artery—Any blood vessel that carries blood away from the heart to the rest of the body.

atria—The two upper chambers of the heart.

barber-surgeons—Members of a profession that, in Harvey's time, both cut hair and performed operations. They had less medical training than physicians.

capillaries—The smallest blood vessels of the body. They connect the smallest arteries to the smallest veins.

cardiology—The study of the heart.

circulation—Movement of the blood in a circular path through the body and lungs, pumped by the heart.

circulatory system—The network of veins, arteries, and capillaries through which blood moves in a circular path through the body.

clot—A thickened mass of blood.

contracting—Squeezing together.

development—The growth of a living thing from the joining of egg and sperm to birth.

dilating—Opening or expanding.

dissect—To cut open and examine.

fetuses—Living things not yet developed enough to be born.

humors—The four body fluids that, according to the ancient Greeks, controlled health and disease. The humors were blood, phlegm or mucus, yellow bile, and black bile. The Greeks believed that too much or too little of a humor could make someone sick.

leaping point—The first part of an unborn chick that moves. It will become the bird's heart.

LVAD (left ventricular assist device)—An invention that takes over the pumping function of a weakened heart.

pacemaker—The bundle of nerves in the right atrium that controls the heartbeat. An artificial pacemaker can take over the job of the natural one if the natural one does not work right.

phlegm—One of the four body fluids or humors. It was similar to what is now called mucus.

physiology—The study of the way parts of living bodies work.

pulmonary artery—The vessel that carries blood from the right ventricle of the heart to the lungs.

pulmonary vein—A vessel that carries blood from the lungs to the left atrium of the heart.

quack—An untrained or poorly trained person who offers medical services.

sperm—The cell from a male that unites with the egg of a female to create a new living thing.

valves—Tiny "doors" in the heart and veins that force blood to flow only in one direction.

veins—Blood vessels that carry blood from the body toward the heart.

venae cavae—The two large veins that bring blood from the body into the right atrium of the heart.

ventricles—The two lower chambers of the heart. They receive blood from the atria and force it out into either the lungs (right ventricle) or the rest of the body (left ventricle).

Further Reading

Books

Cooper, Sharon Katz. *Human Body Systems: Maintaining the Body's Fractions.* Minneapolis, Minn: CompassPoint Books, 2007.

Curry, Don L. *How Does Your Heart Work?* New York: Scholastic/Children's Press, 2004.

Gray, Susan Heinrichs. *The Human Body: The Heart.* Mankato, Minn.: Child's World, 2005.

Simon, Seymour. *The Heart: Our Circulatory System.* New York: Collins, 2006.

Internet Addresses

All About the Heart
http://www.kidshealth.org/kid/body/heart_noSW.html

The Human Heart
http://www.fi.edu/learn/heart/index.html

Circulatory System
http://vilenski.org/science/humanbody/hb_html/circ_system.html

Index

last days of, 95–100
later in life, 55–57
legacy of, 101–107
life at the court, 57–66
Royal College and, 27–32
travels in Europe, 66–70
heart and blood, movement
   of, 36–54
human anatomy, book on, 17
humors, 32

J
Jefferson, Thomas, 74

K
King Charles I, 35, 57
King Henry VIII, 72
King's School, 10

L
Leeuwenhoek, Antonie van,
   102
logic, 13
Lord Denbigh, 70
Lumleian Lectures, 28
Lumley, John, 28
LVAD (left ventricle assist
   device), 111

M
Malphighi, Marcello, 103
Maria, Henrietta, 72
Merton College, 78

N
Newton, Isaac, 102

O
Oxford University, 78
oxygen, 47

P
pacemaker, 43
Parliament, 71
Parr, Thomas, 61
pulmonary artery, 40

Q
Queen Elizabeth I, 25

R
Riolan, Jean, 85
Royal College of Physicians,
   22, 27–32
Royal Society of London, 101

S
sperm, 93
St. Bartholomew's Hospital,
   26
stethoscope, 105

T
Thirty Years' War, 66

U
University of Padua, 15

V
valve, 39
veins, 18, 40
venae cavae, 40
ventricles, 39
Vesalius, Andreas, 16
vital spirit, 48

W
West Dane (farm), 8
witches, 65

Let's Talk!

"Please" and "thank you" might be your friend's first American words. Why? You have used good manners. You have **accepted** your friend just the way she is. Soon your new friend will speak English. Then you need to be a good listener. Hear what she has to say. Share ideas with her. Listen to her ideas.

BAD HELP

Lucy Lee moved to the United States from Korea. She was seven years old. Children at school laughed at her way of talking. One day she needed to tell her teacher something. She asked a boy for help. He taught her bad words. Lucy said the bad words to her teacher. Lucy got in trouble. Now Lucy is a teacher. She understands new kids and their problems.

Learning about Other People and Cultures

Lucy Lee understands new students.

Begin to build **trust**. Tell your friend what you think of a book. Ask her what she thinks. You don't have to think the same way. You don't have to like the same things. You do need to be respectful. Remember the seed in the garden? Seeds grow when they are watered and fed. Friendships grow when you listen, talk, and care!

Learn to share ideas with new friends.

3

Show You Care

Doing the right thing is not always easy. Sometimes it is hard. When new children move near you, take the time to greet them. When there is a disabled child in your class, be kind. Others will be watching you. You are the shining example.

Opposite: The lunchroom should be a happy place. It is where everyone sits together.

friend bring? Ever heard of kimchi? Your friend from North Carolina may bring in grits or cornbread. It's fun to taste and smell new foods.

Decorate the desks in your room with pictures and maps. Ask your teacher to put a big map of the United States on the wall. Everyone in your class can put a dot on the state where they

Find out where your friends are from.

were born. What about your Korean friend? Do the same thing with a map of the world. Think about how Korea is so far away.

Get to know your Korean friend. You can learn about her Korean **culture**. You can begin to understand about her life in Korea. North Carolina is not as far away as Korea. If you live in Ohio, it's still far! Find out how Southern culture is different from culture in the Midwest.

Take time to listen to learn about others.

Talk and Listen

Take time to talk to children who are different from you. They might want to know about you. Think about how you are different. See how you are the same. Draw a picture of your family to share.